Science
Mind
Stretchers

by
Imogene Forte and Sandra Schurr

Incentive Publications, Inc.
Nashville, Tennessee

Cover and illustrations by Maribeth Wright
Edited by Sally D. Sharpe

ISBN 0-86530-165-4

Table Of Contents

ch 13

ch 10

ch 15

ch 8

ch 5

ch 4

HOW TO USE THIS BOOK

Several years ago educators documented the fact that learning occurs in several sequential stages. Each stage of learning has been identified and defined by Benjamin S. Bloom as part of an established taxonomy to encourage teachers to stimulate varied thinking skills in children. These six stages of cognitive development are as follows:

> Knowledge - remembering information
> Comprehension - understanding information
> Application - using information
> Analysis - breaking information into component parts
> Synthesis - putting information together in new ways
> Evaluation - judging information

In developing the science activities in this book, we have used a wide range of learning behaviors and/or trigger verbs from Bloom's Taxonomy to "stretch" the students' minds when learning basic science concepts. For example:

... knowledge science activities - ask students to find definitions, search for information, or answer questions

... comprehension science activities - encourage debates, paraphrasing, and the giving of examples to indicate an understanding of a new scientific idea

... application science activities - involve students in role playing and model building tasks

... analysis science activities - provide opportunities for making deductions, identifying problems, or eliciting comparisons

... synthesis science activities - show students how to solve problems creatively and how to change an idea or product

... evaluation science activities - introduce students to the process of evaluating data, products, ideas

This collection of mini-units and the accompanying reproducible pages in the areas of life, earth, and physical science have been developed to help you extend science concepts and reinforce skill development in the areas of reading, writing, and thinking. Enjoy!

AVIATION

✈ KNOWLEDGE

Draw a simple outline of an airplane. Label the following parts on your diagram:

propeller	stabilizers
landing gear	elevators
wings	rudder
cockpit	flaps
ailerons	fuselage

✈ COMPREHENSION

In your own words, explain how thrust, lift, gravity, and drag make an airplane fly.

✈ APPLICATION

Construct several paper airplane models. Try making them from different materials such as newspaper, waxed paper, construction paper, or wrapping paper. Which fly best?

✈ ANALYSIS

Differentiate the following forms of air transportation by listing similarities and differences or advantages and disadvantages of each: helicopter, dirigible, hot air balloon, parachute, and hang glider.

✈ SYNTHESIS

What would you write if you were the most famous and daring skywriter in the world? Create a picture of examples of your work.

✈ EVALUATION

List all the professions you can think of which have to do with airplanes. Rank them in order of importance. Explain your ranking process.

AVIATION

NAME _____   DATE

Draw a picture of what your neighborhood, house, or community would look like to a person in an airplane.   _____

Predict all the ways you can think of that our lives would be changed if there were no way to fly.   _____

Plan a paper airplane flying contest. Give prizes for airplane entries that:

        can fly the farthest.
        can fly the highest.
        can fly the longest.
        are smallest in size.
        are largest in size.
        are most unusual in design.
        are the most decorative.   _____

THE FIRST AIRPLANE FLIGHT

Try to recall everything you have learned about the flight of the first mechanically-powered airplane. In the space below, write an account of the event. Include information about who designed and flew the plane, where and when the flight took place, and other pertinent facts. Use library resources to check the accuracy of your account. Then, use the back of this paper to rewrite your report, making necessary corrections and adding facts gained from your research.

_____

_____

_____

_____

_____

_____

_____

_____

_____

_____

_____

_____

_____

_____

_____

_____

AIRPLANE DRAMA

Write a brief play from a pilot's point of view about taking an airplane trip. Include information about parts of the airplane, principles of flight, and the roles of different workers on the ground crew.

Outline your play below.

CHARACTERS:

_____

_____

_____

_____

TIME AND PLACE (SETTING):

_____

_____

_____

_____

PROBLEM OR CONFLICT:

_____

_____

_____

_____

SPECIAL WORDS, TERMS, OR PRINCIPLES TO BE INCLUDED:

_____

_____

_____

BATTERIES

 **KNOWLEDGE**

List as many uses as you can think of for household batteries.

 **COMPREHENSION**

Describe the composition of a battery.

 **APPLICATION**

Demonstrate or draw a series of diagrams to illustrate how to properly insert a battery into a flashlight, a transistor radio, a tape recorder, or a traveling alarm clock.

 **ANALYSIS**

Determine ways the battery has changed the following markets:

      toys   small appliances   health aids

 **SYNTHESIS**

Invent a new toy that operates on batteries. Draw your design and indicate how and where the batteries are to be installed.

 **EVALUATION**

What criteria would you set up to evaluate the quality of a particular brand of battery? How would you use this criteria in the selection of your next battery?

BATTERIES

NAME _____ DATE

Use the Yellow Pages of the telephone directory to find the names and locations of five businesses where you can purchase batteries. _____

Demonstrate in a drawing or a short paragraph how batteries are used in any one of the following categories: _____

    home entertainment   communications
    health care   international travel
    law enforcement   ocean exploration _____

Imagine that you are the world's most successful battery salesperson. Develop a creative sales promotion campaign that includes ideas for T.V. commercials, magazine advertisements, and store displays. _____

HOW BATTERIES WORK

Batteries provide the force to move electrons through a wire in order to make electricity. This force is called the electromotive force. The strength of such a force is measured in volts, named after Alessandro Volta, the inventor of the first battery.

A battery is made up of many cells. Each cell contains a liquid called the electrolyte. It is made up of billions of positive and negative particles. When two rods, called electrodes, are submerged in the electrolyte, a chemical reaction takes place. This reaction sends positive particles to one electrode and negative particles to the other. When a wire is connected to the two electrodes, current flows along the wire.

Fill in the blanks below with the number of the answer from the circuit board on the next page. Check your answers by writing the numbers of each answer in the corresponding magic square on page 16. If all answers are correct, you will get 27 when you add down, across, or diagonally.

A. _____ provide the force to move electrons through a wire.

B. This force is called the _____ force.

C. The strength of such a force is measured in _____ .

D. _____ is the inventor of the first battery.

E. A battery is made up of many _____ .

F. The electrolyte liquid is made up of billions of _____ and _____ particles.

G. Two rods, called _____ , cause a chemical reaction to take place when submerged in the electrolyte.

H. A _____ sends positive particles to one electrode and negative particles to another electrode.

I. _____ flows along a wire when the wire is connected to two electrodes.

CIRCUIT BOARD

1. electromotive
3. current
5. Alessandro Volta
7. electrodes
9. cells

11. volts
13. positive, negative
15. batteries
17. chemical reaction

A	B	C
D	E	F
G	H	I

MAGIC SQUARES

BATTERY DILEMMAS

Write a complete sentence to explain what you would do in each of the following situations.

1. Your mother tries to start the family car in order to take you to school but the battery is dead.

   _____

   _____

2. You are preparing to conduct a science experiment involving the use of batteries, but you have forgotten how to wire the batteries correctly.

   _____

   _____

3. You have bought a battery-operated toy for a younger brother or sister and the directions for installing the batteries are missing.

   _____

   _____

4. You are a battery salesperson. You have been asked to write a statement explaining why your product is the best on the market.

   _____

   _____

5. You are on the way to the beach and discover that you do not have batteries for your transistor radio.

   _____

   _____

6. You are ready to leave for a camping trip and can't find the batteries for your flashlight.

   _____

   _____

HOUSEHOLD CURRENTS

Do you ever stop to think how much you and your family depend on electrical currents? In the empty rooms below, draw pictures to show electrical household appliances that are used in your home on a daily basis.

BICYCLE MECHANICS

🚲 KNOWLEDGE

List as many parts of a bicycle as you can. Use each word in a complete sentence to show the basic meaning or function of the bicycle part.

🚲 COMPREHENSION

In your own words, explain how the gear system of a bicycle works.

🚲 APPLICATION

Distinguish among a velocipede, a tandem, and a ten speed bicycle.

🚲 ANALYSIS

Infer how bikes are related to health. Prepare a three minute speech to share your ideas with the class.

🚲 SYNTHESIS

Invent a new way to prevent bicycle theft. Consider such things as locks, warning devices, identification procedures, laws, or self-help programs.

🚲 EVALUATION

Do you think that bicycle riders should be required to pass an operator's test? Summarize your ideas in a one page position paper.

BICYCLE MECHANICS

NAME _____ DATE

Make a list of safety rules that you think would prevent bicycle injuries. _____

If you were responsible for starting a bicycle safety inspection program at your school, what things would you include in your plan? Outline your ideas. _____

Explain how a bicycle illustrates each of the following scientific principles:

      application of force
      friction acting against motion
      acceleration
      low velocity _____

Create a unique bicycle design for each of the following creatures: octopus, spider, giraffe, elephant, penguin. _____

Design an unusual bike trail for one of the following types of cycles: tricycles, unicycles, motorcycles, or bicycles for two. _____

BICYCLES ARE COMPLEX MACHINES

Study the bicycle diagram below. Find at least one representation in the diagram of each of the six simple devices listed below. List the examples below the devices.

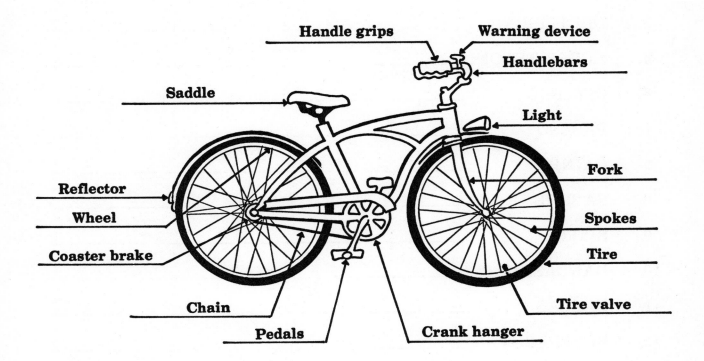

1. Wheel and Axle

_____

_____

2. Screw

_____

_____

3. Lever

_____

_____

4. Pulley

_____

_____

5. Wedge

_____

_____

6. Inclined Plane

_____

_____

Answer key on pages 126 and 127.

BICYCLE SAFETY
WORD SCRAMBLE

Unscramble the words below.

1. SIECPIONTN   _____

2. GSIALN   _____

3. DEETPISRNA   _____

4. NCESRITETONI   _____

5. CIYLBCE   _____

6. PKSESO   _____

7. CAINH   _____

8. SARKBE   _____

9. SPIRG   _____

10. BANLASHDER   _____

11. DEPLAS   _____

12. RCFERLEOT   _____

13. IEBK OTURE   _____

14. ROCSWSKLA   _____

15. AWRGINN GISNS _____

BIKE ROUTE	CROSSWALK
PEDALS	REFLECTOR
BICYCLE	INTERSECTION
INSPECTION	PEDESTRIAN
HANDLEBARS	SPOKES
SIGNAL	WARNING SIGNS
GRIPS	BRAKES
CHAIN	

Answer key on pages 126 and 127.

WHAT'S THE QUESTION?

Think about the bicycle-related terms and ideas below. Write an appropriate question for each answer.

1. **QUESTION:** _____

   _____

   ANSWER: Gears

2. **QUESTION:** _____

   _____

   ANSWER: Bicycle Path

3. **QUESTION:** _____

   _____

   ANSWER: Unicycle

4. **QUESTION:** _____

   _____

   ANSWER: 5 to 10 Speeds

5. **QUESTION:** _____

   _____

   ANSWER: Highway Signs and Traffic Signals

6. **QUESTION:** _____

   _____

   ANSWER: Speedometer

7. **QUESTION:** _____

   _____

   ANSWER: Recreational Benefits of Bicycling

8. **QUESTION:** _____

   _____

   ANSWER: Right of Way

9. **QUESTION:** _____

   _____

   ANSWER: License

10. **QUESTION:** _____

    _____

    ANSWER: High Risers

THE SPORT OF CYCLING

Pretend that you are a cyclist and have been asked to do the following tasks. Write your responses on the provided lines.

TASK ONE

You have been asked to plan a bike-a-thon for your school. What route would you plan for the bike-a-thon?

_____

_____

_____

_____

_____

TASK TWO

You have been asked to plan a six-week training program for junior cyclists. What would the program involve?

_____

_____

_____

_____

_____

TASK THREE

You have been asked to plan a window display for a new bicycle shop that caters to middle graders. What would the display look like?

_____

_____

_____

_____

BODY SYSTEMS

🧫 KNOWLEDGE

Memorize the major systems of the human body. List them in alphabetical order.

🧫 COMPREHENSION

Draw a diagram and use it to explain the major parts and functions of one of the human body systems.

🧫 APPLICATION

Apply what you know about one of the systems of the human body by suggesting a series of activities or procedures that one could regularly practice to maintain proper functioning of that system.

🧫 ANALYSIS

Compare and contrast one of the systems of the human body with that of another organism.

🧫 SYNTHESIS

Write an imaginary story about a . . .

    day in the life of a brain cell
    day in the life of a nerve ending
    day in the life of a red corpuscle
    day in the life of a muscle

🧫 EVALUATION

If you were to become a worldwide expert on one of the human body systems, which would you choose and why?

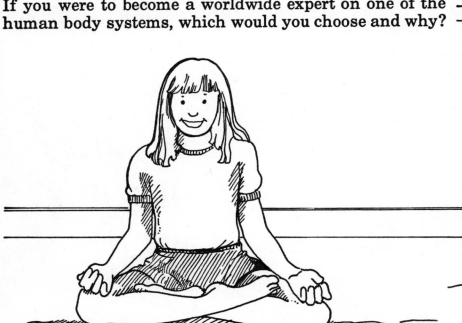

BODY SYSTEMS

NAME _____ DATE

List a disease, ailment, or malfunction for each system of
the human body.   _____

Locate information about an individual who has made a
significant contribution to scientific knowledge of one or
more body systems.   _____

Use your knowledge of the human body systems to defend
this statement:

    Drug, alcohol, and tobacco abuse can cause harmful
    effects to all major functions of the body systems.   _____

BODY SYSTEM EXPERT

Select one of the major body systems that you would like to study. Use the study plan below to research the body system. When your research is complete, use a separate sheet of paper to write a true/false test related to the system. Ask a classmate to take the test. Check the paper and discuss the answers.

Study plan for researching: _____

_____

_____

Some things I want to know: _____

_____

_____

To find answers I will: _____

_____

_____

Resources I will use: _____

_____

_____

To organize my information I will: _____

_____

_____

I will give my true/false test to: _____

_____

_____

DIARY OF A DIET

Do you agree or disagree with the statement "you are what you eat"? Have you thought about how your daily diet affects each of your major body systems?

Use the form below to record everything you eat today. At the end of the day, review the record to see if you had a balanced diet and if the quantity and quality of food was sufficient to properly maintain each of your body systems.

Breakfast	Lunch	Dinner
Estimated calories: _____	Estimated calories: _____	Estimated calories: _____

Snacks	Time eaten	Estimated calories

COLOR

KNOWLEDGE

Make a list of the basic colors. Write other color words that are shades or hues of each basic color.
Example: Green
        a. mint   b. lime   c. chartreuse

COMPREHENSION

People say that colors make them feel either warm or cool. Pick six or seven colors and use each one to color a square of paper. Show the squares, one at a time, to several people. Ask each person whether he or she feels warm, hot, cool, or cold when viewing each color. Graph your results. In a short paragraph, explain the findings of your "research" on warm and cool colors.

APPLICATION

Experiment to find out how many different colors you can create by mixing two or more of these four colors: blue, red, yellow, black. Record your results.

ANALYSIS

Paint or color a picture that is completely yellow. Infer what would happen if everything were yellow. List all of the possible effects.

SYNTHESIS

Using this chart of color meanings, design a coat of arms for your family.

yellow or gold - honor, loyalty   blue - sincerity
     brown - flexibility   orange - strength
       black - grief, sorrow   purple - royalty
      white - faith, purity   green - hope
         red - bravery

EVALUATION

Artists use color to "speak", and poets use color to paint visual word pictures. Scientists view color as something that is partially in the object, partially in the light, and partially in the eye. Determine how three people in different professions can view color very differently. Support your responses with examples.

COLOR

Give examples of several occupations that require a knowledge of color. _____

Use each of these "colorful" expressions in a sentence. Color or paint a picture to show what each expression means. _____

white as a sheet	colorful person
tickled pink	green thumb
sky blue	show one's true colors

What is the best color to represent each of the following? _____

anger	patriotism
fear	friendship
love	illness
happiness	autumn

Justify to someone why you chose the colors that you did. _____

MAKE A SET OF 3-D GLASSES

1. Draw a pair of glasses on heavy paper or cardboard (see the illustration). Cut out the glasses.

2. Paste a piece of red cellophane on the glasses to make the right lens. Paste a piece of green cellophane on the glasses to make the left lens.

3. Draw a picture using a red pencil. On a separate sheet of paper, draw a picture using a green pencil.

4. Put on the glasses. Shut your left eye and look at the red drawing through the red cellophane lens. Then shut your right eye and look at the green drawing through the green cellophane lens. Record what you see in each instance and explain why you think these things occur.

RED LENS
What happens? _____

Why does it happen? _____

GREEN LENS
What happens? _____

Why does it happen? _____

SHOW YOU HAVE AN EYE FOR COLOR

Certain colors complement each other whereas others clash. Show that you have an eye for color by using markers to complete each color task.

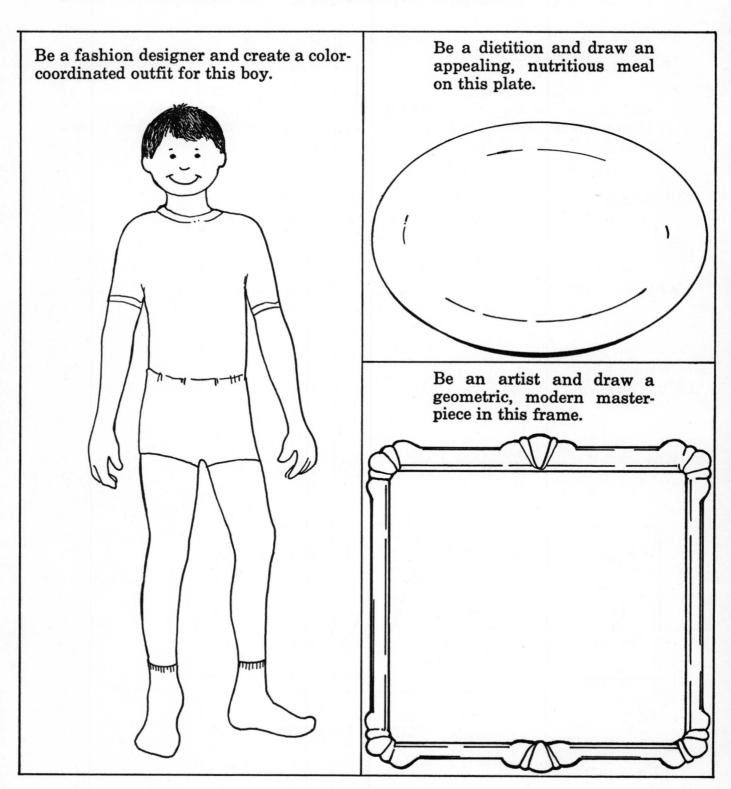

Be a fashion designer and create a color-coordinated outfit for this boy.

Be a dietition and draw an appealing, nutritious meal on this plate.

Be an artist and draw a geometric, modern masterpiece in this frame.

ENDANGERED SPECIES

 KNOWLEDGE

List these endangered species in alphabetical order.

Ceylon elephant   whooping crane   white rhinoceros
snow leopard   spider monkey   Andrean condor

 COMPREHENSION

Give at least ten examples of how human beings have made changes in the environment which in turn have endangered several animal species.

 APPLICATION

Animals provide people with many products – some of which are needs and some of which are wants. Discover what animal gives us each of the following products and whether each product is a want or a need.

gelatin   ivory   bristle   fur
parchment   musk   blubber   glycerin

 ANALYSIS

Choose an endangered species of interest to you. Research to find out why the organism is endangered and how the organism might be saved. Outline a plan of action that could be used to prevent extinction.

 SYNTHESIS

Create a name poem to describe key facts about an endangered species. Choose from these animals: orangutan, armadillo, sloth, manatee, ferret, gazelle, panda, and ocelot.

> S low
> L ong arms
> O dd-looking
> T hree toes
> H airy

 EVALUATION

Pretend you are on the City Council to decide whether a community baseball field/stadium should be built on a large, undisturbed meadow which also serves as a bird and wildlife sanctuary. Prepare a logical argument for or against the field/stadium that might be offered by each of the following individuals. Make a decision based on the logic of the arguments.

wildlife biologist, local bird watcher, baseball player

ENDANGERED SPECIES

NAME _____   DATE

Explain how one or more of the following groups have
worked to protect the world's endangered species.   _____

Park and Forest Rangers   The Sierra Club
The Audubon Society   The International Wildlife
National Wildlife   Federation
  Federation   National Geographic Society

Collect magazine and newspaper articles related to
endangered species. Use the articles to show causes and
effects of human carelessness and indifference.   _____

Design a poster to influence people to contribute to a fund
for the protection of the endangered species of your
choice.   _____

PLAN TO SAVE A LIFE

Select one animal that is in danger of becoming extinct. Use reference materials to complete the work sheet below.

Animal: _____

Reference sources to be used:

1. _____

2. _____

3. _____

Animal's natural habitat: _____

_____

_____

Facts about the animal: _____

_____

_____

Steps that are now being taken to protect the animal: _____

_____

_____

Questions that you have about the protection of the species: _____

_____

_____

WRITE A LETTER TO SHOW THAT YOU CARE

Below are the names and addresses of three organizations devoted to the preservation of animals in danger of extinction. Use the information collected on the "Plan To Save A Life" work sheet to write a letter to one of the organizations. Express your specific concern for an endangered species and ask for more information about the animal as well as suggestions for ways that you can help.

World Wildlife Fund
910 17th Street N.W.
Washington, D.C. 20013

International Union of Conservation
    Of Natural Resources
1110 Murges
Vaud, Switzerland

National Audubon Society
950 Third Avenue
New York, New York 10022

In the box below, design a badge that you can wear to show that you care about the world's endangered species. Make a copy of the badge and use it as a letterhead for the stationery on which you write your letter.

ENVIRONMENT

 KNOWLEDGE

Define the word environment.

 COMPREHENSION

Describe the environment of one or more of the following animals: camel, polar bear, pelican, llama, whale, seal, kangaroo.

 APPLICATION

Collect as much information as you can about the role of an environmentalist. Organize your findings in outline form.

 ANALYSIS

Survey your environment to discover something that . . .
- looks ugly to you.
- looks beautiful to you.
- could be made into a nice gift.
- is important to humans but can't be seen or touched.
- you would like to be.
- your teacher would not like.

 SYNTHESIS

Compose a series of diary entries on this topic: "I travel through outer space and see many environments. Let me describe some of the environments I have seen."

 EVALUATION

Complete the following statement and give details to support your response. If I could change the environment that I live in now, I would change . . .

NAME _____ DATE

What are some important things that the cultural environment (things made by man) and the natural environment (things not made by man) do for us? _____

Debate how a cultural environment is like a natural environment and yet is different from a natural environment. _____

In order for the cultural environment to grow, it must assimilate part of the natural environment. Do you agree or disagree? Justify your response. _____

In your own words, explain how people can be "shaped" by their environments. Is this good or bad? Give examples to justify your ideas. _____

OBSERVATION OUTLOOK

Sometimes people become so accustomed to their own environments that they fail to notice important details. Test your awareness of your school environment by answering each of the questions below with your best estimate. Then check each of your answers for accuracy and write the correct answers in the fact column.

		Estimate	Fact
1.	How many classrooms are there in your school?		
2.	How many miles is it from your home to school?		
3.	How tall is your principal?		
4.	How many doors does the school library have?		
5.	How old is the youngest member of your class?		
6.	What is the average monthly rainfall in the community where your school is located?		
7.	What is the name of the author(s) of your science book?		
8.	What color are your best friend's eyes?		
9.	Does the heating system in your school cause air pollution?		
10.	What is the species of the largest tree on your school's campus?		
11.	How many electric appliances are in use in your classroom?		
12.	How many boys are there in your grade?		
13.	Are there more boys or more girls in your class?		
14.	How many fire extinguishers are there in your school?		

DRAW IT LIKE YOU SEE IT

On a large sheet of paper, draw a picture of your school and the street in front of the school. Include as many details as possible (trees, flag, windows, signs, etc.). Examine your picture carefully for signs of pollution or environmental abuse.

List three things in the school's environment of which you are especially proud.

1.

2.

3.

List three things in the school's environment that you would like to change.

1.

2.

3.

Compare your completed picture and your lists to those of a classmate to find out how many things are the same.

INSECTS

 KNOWLEDGE

Brainstorm and list at least one insect for each letter of the alphabet. Group your list of bugs as good guys or bad guys according to whether they are helpful or harmful insects.

 COMPREHENSION

Choose an insect to research. Make a collection of ten facts about your insect -- five that are true facts and five that are not true facts. Write each fact on a separate file card. Give the cards to a friend and see if he or she can tell fact from fiction.

 APPLICATION

Interview ten people to find out what insect each dislikes the most. Graph the results and draw conclusions from your findings.

 ANALYSIS

Search for the names of insects to finish these similes or comparisons.

As noisy as a . . .   As funny as a . . .
As pesty as a . . .   As unusual as a . . .
As lovely as a . . .   As leggy as a . . .
As tiny as a . . .   As bright as a . . .
As fast as a . . .   As clumsy as a . . .
As popular as a . . .

 SYNTHESIS

Combine parts of several different insects to create a new kind of insect. Draw a picture of the insect and label the parts.

 EVALUATION

If you had to become an insect, which one would you choose to be? Support your choice with at least five reasons.

NAME _____ DATE

Name at least five ways man protects himself from harmful insects. _____

Pretend you are a bug found in your backyard. Write your life story, making certain your ideas are as scientific as possible. _____

   a.   When were you born?
   b.   Where do you live?
   c.   What is your family history?
   d.   What are your hobbies?
   e.   What work do you do?
   f.   Where do you like to travel?
   g.   Who are your friends?
   h.   What special skills or talents do you have?
   i.   What do you look like?

Find a can of insect repellent in your house or a supermarket. Read the information on the can to learn something about the repellent. _____

Invent a new kind of bug spray. Be sure to tell what the bug spray is for and what it will do. Think of a clever name for your repellent and draw a picture to show what your repellent does. _____

How would you draw each of the bugs listed below if you did not know what each bug was but you did know what the words in their names meant? Be creative in your drawings. _____

   Dragonfly   Silverfish
   Yellow Jacket   Walking Stick
   Bedbug

Which insect has the most effect — good, bad, or both — on you and your family? Defend your answer in a detailed paragraph. _____

UNDERCOVER INSECTS

Find and color nine insects hiding in the picture below. Can you name at least five insects that use camouflage as part of their protection?

Answer key on pages 126 and 127.

PUZZLING INSECTS

Find and circle the names of 20 insects in the word find puzzle below. The words may be spelled vertically or horizontally, but not diagonally or backward. Write every leftover letter, except the letters a, b, c, and d in the space below the puzzle. Unscramble the letters to spell the name of a professionally trained person who studies insects.

a	s	i	l	v	e	r	f	i	s	h	b
d	t	u	m	b	l	e	b	u	g	b	c
c	a	p	h	i	d	m	a	o	w	d	a
b	e	e	t	l	e	o	d	c	a	f	t
k	i	d	a	n	t	t	e	g	s	l	e
a	g	r	a	s	s	h	o	p	p	e	r
t	m	a	g	g	o	t	c	b	a	a	m
y	s	g	m	o	s	q	u	i	t	o	i
d	l	o	c	u	s	t	m	a	o	d	t
i	t	n	w	a	t	e	r	b	u	g	e
d	o	f	b	u	t	t	e	r	f	l	y
s	i	l	k	w	o	r	m	n	l	t	a
f	l	y	b	u	m	b	l	e	b	e	e

INSECT SURROUNDINGS

Draw the habitat or natural environment of each insect below. Use reference materials in the library to find information about each insect.

GRASSHOPPER	MOLE CRICKET
TERMITE	**DRAGONFLY**

NAME AN INSECT THAT . . .

Write the name of an insect for each of the characteristics below.

1. An insect that is a music maker

    _____

2. An insect with a powerful jaw for chewing

    _____

3. An insect with a coiled tube for sipping liquids

    _____

4. An insect that is helpful to man

    _____

5. An insect that is a "social" insect

    _____

6. An insect with only two wings

    _____

7. An insect that lays its eggs in or on the water

    _____

8. An insect that molts

    _____

9. An insect without a pupa stage

    _____

10. An insect that is active all year, even where winters are cold

    _____

JUNK FOOD

🍦 KNOWLEDGE

Define the term "junk food" by asking ten of your classmates what the term means to each of them.

🍦 COMPREHENSION

In your own words, summarize the key ingredients that are found in most junk foods.

🍦 APPLICATION

Construct a descriptive pamphlet for your peers to show how junk food can be hazardous to your health.

🍦 ANALYSIS

Go to a local supermarket to discover how junk foods are displayed and where they are located in the store. Draw some conclusions about the effects of the foods' locations and ways of display upon potential customers.

🍦 SYNTHESIS

Design a menu for an imaginary fast food restaurant specializing in burgers and shakes.

🍦 EVALUATION

Many people feel that some foods classified as "junk foods" are very nutritious. Defend this position by writing an editorial that evaluates selected junk foods which are nourishing.

JUNK FOOD

NAME _____   DATE

Write your definition of junk food. Now write the dictionary definition of junk food. How are the definitions alike and how are they different?

_____

Make a list of ten junk foods that you like and ten that you do not like. Arrange each list in alphabetical order.

_____

Using advertisements, wrappers, containers, and samples, make a junk food display. Write a short report about junk foods for the display.

_____

Invent a new junk food to sell to your friends. List the ingredients, design the packaging, create a display case, and give the junk food a catchy name!

_____

Create a series of cartoon strips about the life of a junk food addict.

_____

Assess your eating habits and the quantity of junk food that you eat weekly by keeping a "junk food diary" for one week. Interpret your entries and write a summary at the end of the week.

_____

Critique the foods offered on the menu of a fast food restaurant according to their nutritional values.

_____

JUNK FOOD GUESSING GAME

Estimate how many pieces of the given "junk food" will fit in each geometric shape below. Then fill each shape with the appropriate junk food and count the pieces. Be able to tell which of the junk foods have a real nutritional value and which do not.

M & M's

peanuts

Estimation _____

Actual Number _____

Estimation _____

Actual Number _____

kernels of popcorn

sugar-coated cereal

Estimation _____

Actual Number _____

Estimation _____

Actual Number _____

KICKING THE JUNK FOOD HABIT

Think of a fact, figure, or fictional story about food that each character below might share in order to help kids kick the junk food habit.

METRIC MEASURE

 KNOWLEDGE

List five to ten facts you know about the metric system.

 COMPREHENSION

Draw, demonstrate, write or give an explanation of how the millimeter, centimeter, and decimeter are related to one another.

 APPLICATION

Use a meter stick to measure the length of five objects in the room. Express the length of each item in millimeters, centimeters, and decimeters.

 ANALYSIS

Examine your science textbook to determine how important the metric system is to the study of science.

 SYNTHESIS

Create a slogan to promote widespread use of the metric system in your community.

 EVALUATION

Do you feel that your country should use the metric or the English system of measurement in its activities? What criteria will you set to make your recommendation, and how many reasons can you give to validate your recommendation?

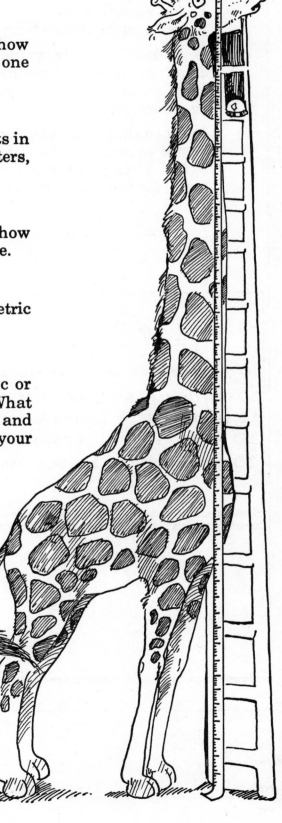

METRIC MEASURE

NAME _____

DATE

List at least five sources from which information about the metric system can be found.

_____

Organize a debate to determine the advantages and disadvantages of using the metric system rather than the English system of measurement for food preparation, currency, and manufacturing.

_____

Create a simple test to determine how much people know or do not know about the metric system. Administer your test to five to ten people and graph the results. Prepare a study guide for the people who made a low score on your test.

_____

Metric System

10 MILLIMETERS = 1 CENTIMETER
10 CENTIMETERS = 1 DECIMETER
10 DECIMETERS = 1 METER
10 METERS = 1 DECAMETER
10 DECAMETERS = 1 HECTOMET

English System

12 INCHES = 1 FOOT
3 FEET = 1 YARD
5½ YARDS = 1 ROD
1,760 YARDS = 1 MILE
3 MILES = 1 LEAGUE

METRIC MASTERY

Use resource books to write a paragraph explaining the metric system and its use. Give examples of three countries in which the metric system is the most used system of measurement.

_____

_____

_____

_____

_____

_____

_____

Write the abbreviation for each metric measurement.

____ centiliter	____ gram	____ meter
____ centimeter	____ hectogram	____ milligram
____ decaliter	____ kilogram	____ millimeter
____ deciliter	____ liter	____ myriameter

Compare and contrast the metric system with the English system of measurement.

Metric System	English System

Answer key on pages 126 and 127.

MEASURE UP

Use a meter stick to measure the following items in meters, decimeters, and centimeters. Then measure each object in yards, feet and inches.

Object	Metric Measurement	English Measurement
your desk		
your height		
your best friend's height		
your science book		
your notebook		
your pencil		
your teacher's desk		
width of your classroom		
length of your classroom		
your index finger		

MICROSCOPES

KNOWLEDGE

Find five objects that you would like to look at under your microscope. Write one fact about each object that you discovered while using your microscope. Draw a picture to show what each object looked like under your microscope.

COMPREHENSION

Extend these starter ideas about microscopes.
    A microscope is important because...
    A microscope can be used for...
    A microscope must never be...

APPLICATION

Water can do interesting things, optically speaking. For this experiment you will need one 3" x 3" square of aluminum foil, a straight pin, and water. Make a small hole in the center of the foil. Drop a small amount of water into the hole. Place an object under the foil and examine the object.

Is the object magnified?
How does the water compare to the lens in a microscope?
If you use a larger hole and a larger drop of water, will the
    magnification increase?
Will other liquids such as vinegar or oil give the same
    magnification results?
Record your findings.

ANALYSIS

Discover all of the ways your microscope is like...
        a pair of glasses.
        a pair of eyes.
        a pair of mirrors.
Share your ideas in writing.

SYNTHESIS

Pretend that you are a microscope. Imagine what you would say to a bug, a mirror, and a scientist.

EVALUATION

Pretend that you have been given the money to buy one of the following pieces of equipment for yourself or your science class. (Assume that you do not have any of these items.) Determine which item you would buy. Justify your choice with three to five reasons.

telescope	periscope
microscope	spectroscope

MICROSCOPES

NAME _____ DATE

If you had to draw a microscope so that someone else would recognize it, would you draw it from the front or from the side? Try drawing a microscope both ways.

_____

Examine several of the following items with a microscope: dust, cloth fibers, sand, paper, soil, yarn, toothpicks, rocks, onionskin, money, fingernails.

_____

When working with your microscope, keep a record of your findings on file cards. Include each of the following on your cards.

_____

Examination number...   Where I found the
Date of examination...   object ...
Object examined...   Illustration of what I saw...
What I saw...   Remarks...

Design a get well card for a broken microscope.

_____

MICRO MANIA

Use the words in the word box to label the parts of the microscope below.

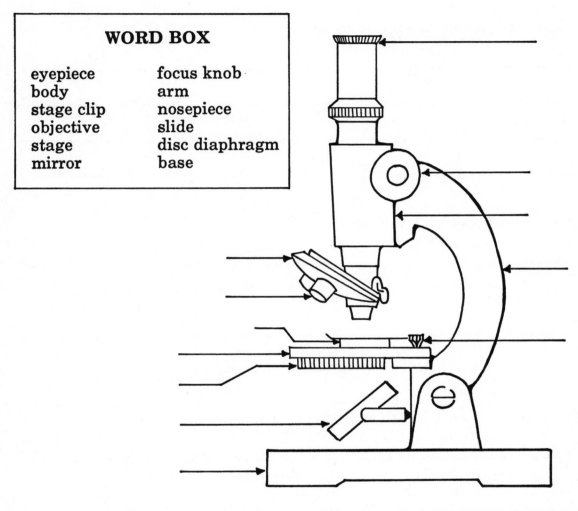

WORD BOX

eyepiece	focus knob
body	arm
stage clip	nosepiece
objective	slide
stage	disc diaphragm
mirror	base

1. Look up the word "micro" in the dictionary and write its definition below.

_____

2. Look up the word "scope" in the dictionary and write its meaning below.

_____

3. In your own words define microscope.

_____

4. Make up some "micro'" words of your own and write their definitions below.

_____

Answer key on pages 126 and 127.

MICRO THINKING

The invention of the microscope was a great thing. Complete the "What If" statements below to share your own thoughts on the subject.

What if the human eye was like a microscope?

_____

_____

_____

_____

What if microscopes were "a dime a dozen"?

_____

_____

_____

_____

What if microscopes allowed you to see into the workings of the mind?

_____

_____

_____

_____

What if microscopes had never been invented?

_____

_____

_____

_____

OCEAN

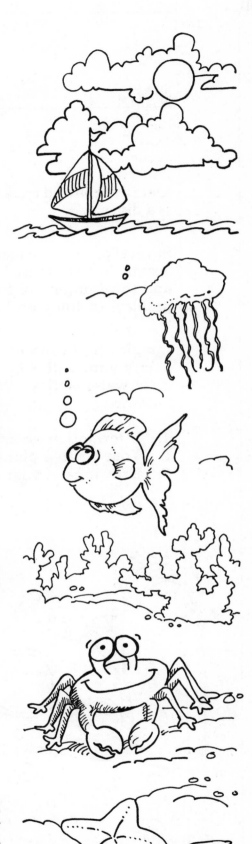

🐚 KNOWLEDGE
Find pictures in magazines that illustrate ideas and facts about the ocean. Some possible concepts include:

Winds cause waves.
Waves can shape beaches.
The moon pulls on the earth to cause the tides.

🐚 COMPREHENSION
Use each of the following ocean-related words in a sentence in order to convey its meaning.

salinity	marine	seaweed
continental	tides	brine
slope	oceanographer	coast
currents	ocean floor	

🐚 APPLICATION
Construct a series of word problems with subjects relating to the ocean. For example: a family harvests 500 pounds of seaweed a week. Thirty percent is sold to a processing plant to be made into medicine and 40 percent is sold to a local market. How many pounds does the family have left to eat?

🐚 ANALYSIS
Many people may live in underwater cities in the future. Draw or write a series of generalizations about the changes in the types of clothing, methods of travel, types of recreational activities, and kinds of foods in such an environment.

🐚 SYNTHESIS
Invent a species of fish that. . .
lies on the bottom of the ocean in sand or mud
eats clams and other shell organisms
escapes capture by jumping and gliding over the
water's surface

🐚 EVALUATION
You are about to take a long ocean voyage in a handcrafted sailboat. Since space is limited, you will be able to take only four of the following items: blanket - oar - first-aid kit - life preserver - anchor - compass - friend. Which items will you take with you and why.

NAME _____   DATE

List the pros and cons of having a porpoise work as a deep-sea diver.

_____

Several problems cause or contribute to the pollution of the ocean. Some of these include oil spills, sewage, pesticides, and the dumping of toxic wastes. Select an ocean-related problem to study and record your findings.

_____

Imagine that you were asked to be part of a group to design a city under the ocean. Begin by doing research on underwater cities. Write a report that includes the following:

_____

1. Information about underwater cities
2. Your written plans for an underwater city
3. Drawings of your underwater city

WHALES, TALES, AND OTHER MYSTERIES OF THE DEEP

Test your knowledge of ocean life by writing the letter of the correct definition beside each term.

A. the only ocean mammals that still have true hind legs with webbed toes

B. an edible fish of the North Atlantic with a greenish, blue-striped back and a silvery belly

1. _____ squids

C. friendly and playful animals that often play near passing ships and that communicate with each other through sharp chirps and squeaks

2. _____ Portuguese man-of-war

D. an animal that has hair, gives birth to young, is warmblooded, and lives on mother's milk during infancy

3. _____ blubber

4. _____ trilobite

E. animals with the same characteristics that can mate and produce young

5. _____ flukes

F. a marine predator that kills its victims by slashing them with a snout edged with sharp teeth

6. _____ sea otters

G. long, slender, fish-eating sea mollusks having ten arms

7. _____ sea cows

8. _____ species

H. a warm-sea siphonophore having a large, bladder-like sac which enables it to float on the water and long tentacles with powerful stinging cells

9. _____ mammal

I. any of several sea mammals in the order Sirenia such as the dugong and manatee

10. _____ mackerel

11. _____ dolphins

J. a sea floor scavenger that is now extinct

12. _____ sawfish

K. layer of fat under the skin of many marine mammals

Answer key on pages 126 and 127.

L. two large fins at the end of a whale's tail

PROTECTION PLEASE

Select one marine animal that is near extinction. Use reference books to find information about the animal. Organize the information below. Then design a poster to encourage protection of the animal.

Animal: _____

REFERENCES: Title   Author   Copyright   Pages

_____

_____

_____

HABITAT: _____

_____

_____

HISTORY: _____

_____

_____

BEHAVIOR: _____

_____

_____

OTHER: _____

_____

_____

ORGAN TRANSPLANTS

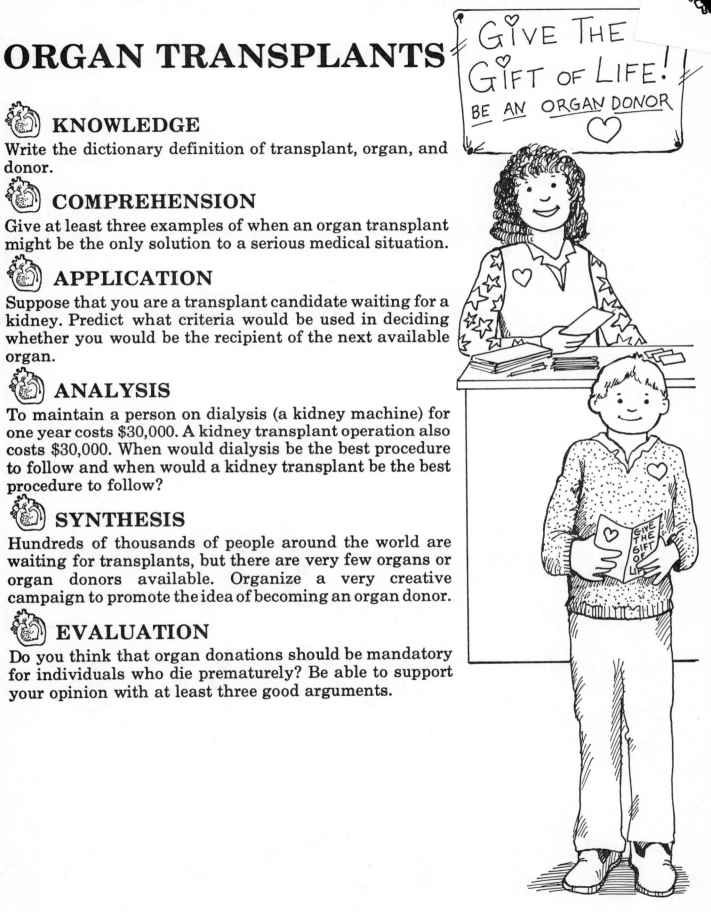

 KNOWLEDGE

Write the dictionary definition of transplant, organ, and donor.

 COMPREHENSION

Give at least three examples of when an organ transplant might be the only solution to a serious medical situation.

 APPLICATION

Suppose that you are a transplant candidate waiting for a kidney. Predict what criteria would be used in deciding whether you would be the recipient of the next available organ.

 ANALYSIS

To maintain a person on dialysis (a kidney machine) for one year costs $30,000. A kidney transplant operation also costs $30,000. When would dialysis be the best procedure to follow and when would a kidney transplant be the best procedure to follow?

 SYNTHESIS

Hundreds of thousands of people around the world are waiting for transplants, but there are very few organs or organ donors available. Organize a very creative campaign to promote the idea of becoming an organ donor.

 EVALUATION

Do you think that organ donations should be mandatory for individuals who die prematurely? Be able to support your opinion with at least three good arguments.

ORGAN TRANSPLANTS

NAME _____   DATE

Make a list of body organs which can be transplanted.   _____

Why are organ transplants often called "the gift of life" or "an ordinary miracle"?   _____

Pretend that you are to interview a potential organ donor. Design interview questions and answers to demonstrate how one goes about becoming an organ donor.   _____

Compare what is involved in a cornea transplant with what is involved in a liver transplant. Show your findings in outline form.   _____

Design a donor card for organ donors. What information would you need or want to know about a donor?   _____

SPARE PARTS FOR PEOPLE

Would you like to meet a bionic boy or girl? Perhaps you already have! The word "bionic" describes any artificial body part that's designed to work exactly like the real thing. Today there are many people whose worn-out or damaged body parts have been replaced by artificial ones.

Pretend that you are a bionic boy or girl living in the year 2050. Write an autobiography telling about your bionic body and your life. The outline below will help you.

Date and place of birth: _____

List of damaged or worn-out body parts and causes of problems:

_____

_____

_____

List of electronic parts or organs obtained:

_____

_____

_____

List of unusual facts, activities, interests and hobbies relating to your mechanical body parts:

_____

_____

_____

LETTERS TO THE EDITOR

Someday doctors will have the medical knowledge enabling them to transplant organs of any type to recipients of any age or sex. Write a letter to the editor describing your feelings, concerns, and expectations surrounding the extensive use of organ transplant banks.

Dear Editor,

THE BUSINESS OF ORGAN TRANSPLANTS

You have been hired to improve the operation of a human organ transplant bank. Write a description of the improvements you plan to make in each of the following areas.

Procedures for organ donors:

_____

_____

_____

_____

Procedures for organ recipients:

_____

_____

_____

_____

Procedures for organ storage, identification and transportation:

_____

_____

_____

_____

Procedures for marketing organ transplant services:

_____

_____

_____

_____

SCIENCE FAIR FUN

Plan a project for the science fair on organ transplants. Combine creative flair with scientific facts to create an outstanding exhibit. Use the questions below as a guide in structuring your project.

From what sources will you get your facts and information?

_____

_____

_____

_____

What type of project will you prepare? (notebook, filmstrip, diorama, model, poster, etc.)

_____

_____

What kind of graphics and illustrations will you use? (charts, graphs, lists, original drawings, pictures, etc.)

_____

_____

_____

How will you evaluate your project? _____

_____

_____

_____

_____

PLANTS

 KNOWLEDGE

Draw several illustrations which show how to grow a particular type of plant. Label your diagrams.

 COMPREHENSION

Make a dictionary to define common terms associated with plants. Give examples with each term.

 APPLICATION

Pretend that you own a valuable species of house plant. One day you discover the plant is wilting and looks very unhealthy. Think of ten things that you might do to save your plant.

 ANALYSIS

Compare a plant to a child, a factory, and a community.

 SYNTHESIS

Plan and organize a special plant show. Who can enter? What categories of plants will you display? How will you judge the entries? What prizes will you give?

 EVALUATION

Conclude what our life and our economy would be like if we were allowed to grow only edible plants. All flowers, house plants, and decorative plants would be forbidden.

NAME _____ DATE

Suppose that someone has given you an unlimited budget to plant a garden. Explain what plants, tools, and chemicals you will need and how you will arrange the plants.

_____

Perform an unusual science experiment using plants. Write your results in scientific form.

_____

Decide what plant would best "describe" your personality. Support your choice with examples.

_____

Many plants have unusual names such as pansy, black-eyed Susan, bleeding heart, and buttercup. Think of several other plants with unusual names and illustrate each one in a creative way.

_____

MYSTERIES OF
THE PLANT WORLD

The plant world is filled with mysteries and "stranger than fiction" facts. Match each plant to its related mysterious fact by writing the letter of the correct fact in the blank beside the corresponding plant.

PLANTS

1. _____ luminous toadstools

2. _____ trumpet plant

3. _____ slime mold

4. _____ orange lichens

5. _____ dodder

6. _____ Indian pipe

7. _____ blue orchid

8. _____ black walnut

9. _____ Spanish moss

10. _____ mistletoe

Answer key on pages 126 and 127.

FACTS

A. gets all of its organic food and minerals from fungi growing underground

B. a parasite with no true roots which robs the host plant of water

C. spreads a poison through the soil around its roots which keeps plants away

D. native to tropical forests; look normal by day but glow mysteriously in the dark

E. a bromeliad with no roots of any kind, no water storage tissues or humus collection power; totally dependent on rain

F. traps and devours insects in a tapering pitcher-like blossom

G. animal-like during growth, but becomes plant-like with spore cases during the reproductive phase

H. has no true leaves or roots; winds threads around a host plant to supply itself with food

I. part fungi, part algae; live on bare rocks in the arctic

J. rare plant of the Amazon basin; its roots hold fast to humus in crevices of tree bark

Select one of the above plants to research. On a separate sheet of paper, draw a picture of the plant showing details of the "stranger than fiction" facts related to its habitat and survival.

THE SPICE OF LIFE

Poetry, prose, art, music, history, ocean journeys, world exploration, business empires, and diets have been influenced over the ages by the quest for new and exotic herbs and spices. Spices have always been prized for their wonderful smells, tastes, and "extraordinary" qualities.

Some spices are derived from the bark of trees, some from plant leaves or fruit, and some from bulbs. Use reference materials to find information about the spices below. Check the appropriate box to show the source of each. Then draw a small picture of the herb or spice.

Herb or Spice	Picture	Bulb	Leaves	Bark	Fruit
Nutmeg					
Dill					
Parsley					
Cinnamon					
Mint					
Red pepper					
Cloves					
Ginger					
Garlic					

PREDATORS AND PREY

 KNOWLEDGE

Record the definitions of predator and prey.

 COMPREHENSION

Predators catch prey by using a variety of adaptations.
Name a different predator for each of these adaptations.

superb eyesight	silence	persistence
muscular power	speed	patience
strong jaws	agility	camouflage

 APPLICATION

Select an animal that uses camouflage as part of its
protection such as a lizard, butterfly, or grasshopper. Draw
a picture to show the environment in which the animal
might hide. Then add the animal to the picture. Next, think
of a likely predator for the animal you have drawn and add
it to the picture.

 ANALYSIS

Study each of the following animals and draw conclusions
as to what adaptations/characteristics make each an
effective predator or a susceptible prey: antelope, armadillo,
skunk, squid, opossum, porcupine.

 SYNTHESIS

Create a super hero/heroine who is named after a well-
known predator. List this person's special powers and
characteristics. Design a costume that "fits" the name you
have chosen.

EVALUATION

In your opinion, what is the world's most successful
predator? Summarize your choice in a good paragraph.

PREDATORS AND PREY

NAME _____ DATE

Pick a common predator and one of its prey. Use a reference book to locate five facts that describe the predator and five facts that describe the prey. Sketch the basic shape of each creature on a sheet of paper. Then write all or some of your factual statements around each animal's shape.

_____

Food chains often involve predators and prey. For example, animals may eat plants or plant-eating animals. Make a food chain to show selected predator/prey relationships.

_____

Design an original game called PREY or PREDATOR.

_____

BOTH PREDATOR AND PREY

The ocean is a constant battlefield for predators and prey. Every living creature fights for survival each day. An animal may be prey for a predator, but it may also be a predator for prey of its own.

Use resource books to find information explaining how the following predators trap their prey.

1. Octopus: _____

    _____

2. Sea anemone: _____

    _____

3. Sea urchin: _____

    _____

4. Triggerfish: _____

    _____

5. Angler fish: _____

    _____

Use resource books to find information explaining how the following prey protect themselves from their predators.

1. Barracuda: _____

    _____

2. Grouper: _____

    _____

3. Jellyfish: _____

    _____

4. Lantern fish: _____

    _____

5. Lobster: _____

    _____

HIDDEN PREY

Find and color the following animals hiding in the picture below.

mouse   frog   rooster   worm   rabbit   deer   chipmunk   fly

Then draw a line from each prey to a predator from which it could be hiding. Some animals may be hiding from more than one predator, so select the predator that you think would be most likely seeking each prey.

Draw pictures to add one more predator and its prey to the picture.

Answer key on pages 126 and 127.

PREHISTORIC LIFE

KNOWLEDGE

Define each of the following words:

prehistoric	fossil
paleontologist	fossil fuel
herbivorous	carnivorous

COMPREHENSION

Explain the adaptive or defensive features and structural characteristics of dinosaurs.

APPLICATION

Construct a series of "Who Am I" cards by describing several different species of dinosaurs on 3" by 5" index cards.

ANALYSIS

Devise a theory to explain why dinosaurs became extinct. Predict how things would be different today if the dinosaurs had lived.

SYNTHESIS

Pretend that you are a paleontologist and have just uncovered the bones of an unknown species of dinosaur. Write a journal entry to describe when and where the bones were found, what you named the dinosaur, what the dinosaur probably looked like, and approximately how big the dinosaur was. Draw a diagram of the dinosaur.

EVALUATION

Set up a list of criteria to use in assessing at least five books about dinosaurs to determine which book is the best reference for your class. Write a paragraph summary of your conclusions.

PREHISTORIC LIFE

NAME _____   DATE

List ten dinosaur names and learn to spell each one.   _____

Explain three major differences in how plant-eating dinosaurs and meat-eating dinosaurs lived.   _____

Make a scrapbook about the plant and animal life of prehistoric times.   _____

Classify each of the ten dinosaurs that you listed according to size, habitat, and food source (plant or animal).   _____

Imagine that you are a scientist preparing to study prehistoric life. Make a list of the tools, equipment, and special reference materials that you will need.   _____

Summarize what you have learned about prehistoric life by writing a feature article suitable for publication in your local newspaper. Be sure to use accurate facts and to organize your information so that the article is easy to read and understand.   _____

DINOSAURS IN HIDING

Five dinosaurs are hiding in the picture below. Find and color the dinosaurs and write each dinosaur's name underneath the picture.

Select the dinosaur that interests you most and write a report about it. Write the report so that it could be used as an article for a natural history magazine. Be sure to include complete bibliographical information for all reference materials used.

Answer key on pages 126 and 127.

DINOSAURS CAN BE PUZZLING

Solve this puzzle to find the "state" of dinosaurs today. To find the hidden word, carefully read each sentence below. If the statement is true, color the numbered spaces as directed. If the statement is false, color nothing.

1. If the scientific name of a person who studies plants and animals of the past is paleontologist, color the #1 spaces.

2. If Pteranodon was a winged reptile that soared through the air, color the #2 spaces.

3. If Stegosaurus was fast and slender, color the #3 spaces.

4. If Protoceratops is known as the "egg-laying dinosaur", color the #4 spaces.

5. If Tyrannosaurus was a huge, fierce, meat-eating creature, color the #5 spaces.

6. If Plesiosaurus lived in caves, color the #6 spaces.

7. If some dinosaurs are still living in jungles of the Amazon, color the #7 spaces.

8. If Anatosaurus is known as the "duck-billed dinosaur", color the #8 spaces.

9. If Diplodocus was a small, meat-eating creature, color the #9 spaces.

ROBOTS

 KNOWLEDGE

List the advantages and the disadvantages of having a robot at home.

 COMPREHENSION

Describe a situation for each of the following categories in which robots have played an important part.

> industry   space   movies

 APPLICATION

Imagine that you are in command of your very own robot. Select a function that you would like to have your robot perform. Use some or all of the terms below to issue commands for completing the function.

lift	lower
move	carry
turn	walk
right	left
up	down
forward	backward

 ANALYSIS

Draw conclusions about the effects that robots could have on your life as you complete these sentences:

1. If I could have a personal robot that I could program to do anything, it would . . .
2. With the time I could save by having my robot work for me, I would . . .
3. I would not like my robot to . . . because . . .

 SYNTHESIS

Many people have lost their jobs as a result of automation. Pretend this has happened to you and write a paragraph explaining how you feel and what you plan to do.

 EVALUATION

You are trying to convince the school board to spend a large sum of money on robots. The board members want to know how robots can be beneficial to the schools. Present your arguments in a speech to your class.

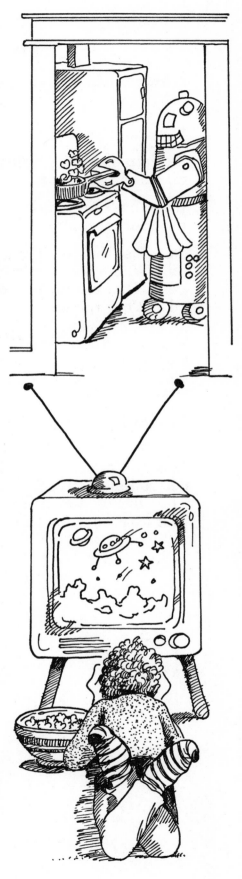

ROBOTS

NAME _____ DATE _____

Draw a picture of a robot. Label the "body" parts. _____

Explain how one can determine whether or not a particular machine is a robot. _____

If the use of robots increases in the future, there will be a need for mechanical doctors. _____

    a. List the qualifications that a robot doctor will need.
    b. Where will a robot doctor receive training?
    c. What robotic ailments will need treatment?
    d. What robotic ailments will be most expensive?

The tin man in THE WIZARD OF OZ was a "robot" who was searching for a heart. Write your own version of this story in which a robot is searching for another human characteristic. _____

Design a business card for a robot repair shop, a robot manufacturer, or a robot service center. _____

Make a list of ten unpleasant jobs or careers. Be sure to determine criteria for what makes a job unpleasant.
Then decide what three jobs on your list could be served best by robots. Justify your choices. _____

CONSTRUCT A ROBOT

Make a robot with odds and ends from around the house. You can make the body with a large, cardboard box and the head with a box that has a plastic colander on top. Cardboard tubes can become arms and legs, and rubber gloves and rubber boots can be hands and feet. You can also make panels for your robot using pieces of corrugated cardboard and small plastic boxes. Egg cartons, bottle tops, margarine tubs, and ping pong balls make great knobs and dials. For the finishing touch, paint your robot any color you choose!

Draw a picture in the space below of what your robot creation might look like. Give your robot a special name!

FROM MACHINES TO ROBOTS

Plan a shopping center for the 21st century. Draw a picture of the shopping center below, showing how robots will provide most of the required services.

DOT-TO-DOT ROBOT

Connect the dots from 1 to 91 to find a most unusual robot. Add details of your own to make the robot uniquely yours.

On another sheet of paper, write a program that would allow the robot to perform a service that would make your life easier or more fun.

Robot's name: _____

LIGHTS! CAMERA! ACTION!

Pretend that you are the writer and producer for a national television station. You have been asked to write and produce a one-hour science fiction production with a cast of three robots and two human beings. The setting is to be New York City in the year 2008. Develop a plot and outline the script. Include the names of all of the characters as well as specifications for costumes, scenery, and special sound effects.

Title: _____

_____

_____

_____

_____

_____

_____

_____

_____

_____

_____

_____

_____

_____

_____

_____

ROCKS AND MINERALS

🪨 **KNOWLEDGE**

Make a list of all the ways you can think of that people change the earth's surface.

🪨 **COMPREHENSION**

Explain how different rocks and minerals are formed.

🪨 **APPLICATION**

Draw a series of three pictures to illustrate commonly used products which are made from rocks and minerals.

🪨 **ANALYSIS**

Do you think there are rocks and minerals on other planets? Explain your answer.

🪨 **SYNTHESIS**

Write a story about a plant or tree "cracking" a great boulder.

🪨 **EVALUATION**

Determine how the minerals of the ocean may be divided fairly among the countries of the world. Make notes for a five minute speech to justify your plans.

ROCKS AND MINERALS

NAME _____ DATE

Collect ten rocks and identify each one according to how it was formed.

_____

Arrange the ten rocks in a display to share with your class. Label each rock and write a brief description of the rock's characteristics and origin.

_____

Develop a plan that you would use if you were going on a rock and mineral expedition. Include what you would take, where you would go, what tasks you would accomplish, and what problems you might encounter.

_____

Write an obituary for a rock. Include where and how the rock was "born", the important events of the rock's "life", and how the rock met its "end".

_____

Compare and contrast the importance of a rock as seen through the eyes of an artist, a geologist, and a gem merchant.

_____

CRYSTAL   DOLOMITE   SLATE

SANDSTONE   GRANITE   FLINT

ROCK-A-ROUND

Complete the crossword puzzle.

ACROSS

2. the most valuable rock of all
3. a rock you burn
6. a record of prehistoric animals or plants
7. rocks formed when molten material cools
12. rocks formed by volcanoes

DOWN

1. sand grains cemented together
4. a rock used for bathtubs
5. a hole in the earth from which hot rock pours
8. the scientist who studies rocks
9. rocks broken down into tiny pieces
10. a rock you eat
11. a sedimentary rock

Write sentence definitions for each of the following terms.

1. igneous rocks _____

2. metamorphic rocks _____

3. sedimentary rocks _____

Answer key on pages 126 and 127.

HOUSEHOLD SURVEY

Draw pictures below to show three rocks or minerals in your home. Write the use or purpose of each one below the picture.

Make an X in the corner of the box of the most expensive one.

Make a O in the corner of the box of the most useful one.

Make a △ in the corner of the box of the one you use most often.

Name _____	Name _____	Name _____
Use _____	Use _____	Use _____

On a separate sheet of paper, design a new household product to be made from rock. Tell the kind of rock it will be made from, what its use will be, and the approximate cost of the product.

SENSES

 KNOWLEDGE

What would you FEEL, SEE, HEAR, SMELL, and TASTE at the bakery, florist, and garage?

 COMPREHENSION

Show how the sense of taste and the sense of smell are related.

 APPLICATION

Make a model of the manual alphabet, Braille alphabet, and Morse code. Demonstrate how each one is used.

 ANALYSIS

Use an ink pad to take the fingerprints of at least ten different classmates. Analyze the thumb prints to determine which classmates have a loop, a whorl, or an arch print.
Record your findings in graph form.

 SYNTHESIS

Create an original "SENSE-SATIONAL" greeting card that emphasizes the sense of touch, the sense of hearing, the sense of smell, or the sense of taste.

 EVALUATION

If you had to lose your sense of sight or your sense of hearing, which one would you want to lose? Defend your choice with at least three to five good reasons.

SENSES

NAME _____   DATE

Name the five senses. Next, make an alphabetical listing of things you can FEEL, SEE, HEAR, SMELL, and TASTE.   _____

Describe how your five senses might help you survive a fire, an earthquake, a tornado, or a hurricane.   _____

Explain what is meant by an optical illusion. Draw an example for your explanation.   _____

Illustrate the parts of an eye and the parts of an ear.   _____

Determine which animal has the best sense of touch, the best sense of sight, the best sense of hearing, the best sense of taste, and the best sense of smell.   _____

Plan a "sensory fair". What unusual activities, projects, and experiments might you have to display at your fair? How might you attract someone to attend your fair by catering to his or her sense of smell, taste, sight, or touch?   _____

If you were hiring an individual for each of the following positions, which one of the five senses would you want to be each individual's strongest asset?   _____

1. Heart Surgeon   6. Newspaper Reporter
2. Hockey Player   7. Restaurant Chef
3. Seamstress   8. Airplane Pilot
4. Watch Repairman   9. Orchestra Conductor
5. Piano Tuner   10. Florist

THE EYES HAVE IT

Use the words in the word box to label the parts of the eye.

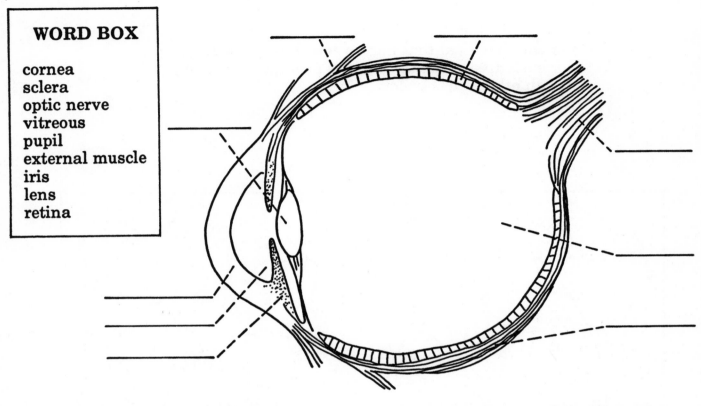

WORD BOX

cornea
sclera
optic nerve
vitreous
pupil
external muscle
iris
lens
retina

List ten tasks that you have completed today that could not have been completed by a person with severely impaired vision.

1. _____

2. _____

3. _____

4. _____

5. _____

6. _____

7. _____

8. _____

9. _____

10. _____

Answer key on pages 126 and 127.

SENSES IN COLOR

Color each area red that names something you can smell.
Color each area green that names something you can hear.
Color all other areas yellow.

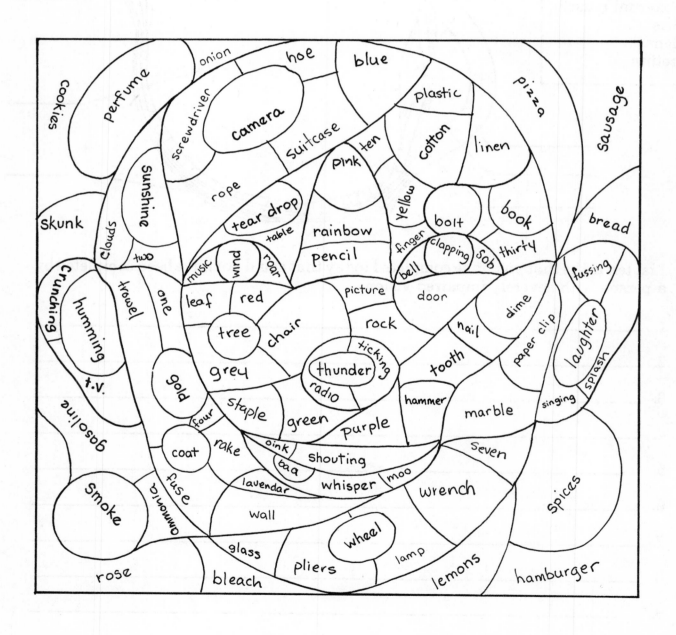

SPACE

⭐⭐ KNOWLEDGE
Draw diagrams of the twelve constellations which are called the zodiac.

⭐⭐ COMPREHENSION
Many planets are named after gods and goddesses from mythology. Explain why you think these names were chosen.

⭐⭐ APPLICATION
Make a drawing to illustrate at least ten different facts about the planets.

⭐⭐ ANALYSIS
You are one of an eight-person astronaut team on an interplanetary space mission. On your return to earth you run into problems and have to leave your craft. Each astronaut lands on a different part of the United States. For each astronaut, form generalizations about the area in which the landing takes place.

Area 1:	Alaska	Area 5:	Florida Everglades
Area 2:	Arizona	Area 6:	Hawaii
Area 3:	Maine	Area 7:	Nebraska
Area 4:	New York City	Area 8:	Texas

⭐⭐ SYNTHESIS
Write an original science fiction story about an expedition to the moon.

⭐⭐ EVALUATION
Many people believe there is life on other planets which is much more sophisticated and advanced than the life on Earth. Describe how you feel about this and try to justify your ideas with important facts and figures.

95

SPACE

Reproduce a chart giving important facts about the planets. _____

Explain how a star is formed. _____

Illustrate several different constellations by creating a mini-planetarium with a light box, flashlight, or diorama. _____

Compare and contrast any two planets in outline form. _____

Create a résumé to convince the people at NASA that you should be the first student in outer space. What subjects, hobbies, work experiences, school activities, and personal characteristics make you a good candidate? _____

Develop a set of recommendations to Congress to encourage more space exploration. Be sure to justify your ideas with logic and facts. _____

WHAT WILL THE FUTURE HOLD?

It is hard to realize that even 50 years ago most people did not believe that man would walk on the moon in this century. Write a story describing how you think space exploration will develop in the next 50 years. Be as imaginative as possible, but include factual details and historical data to make your story interesting and believable.

_____

_____

_____

_____

_____

_____

_____

_____

_____

_____

_____

_____

_____

_____

_____

_____

TEN QUESTIONS

Select the astronaut from the list below who is of the most interest to you. Pretend that you have been selected to interview this astronaut in order to write a television documentary titled "The Lives and Times of America's Astronauts". Develop a list of ten questions that you would ask in order to gather material for the script. Remember, you can ask only ten questions, so plan very carefully in order to get all of the needed information.

Alan Shepard, Jr.   Walter Schirra, Jr.   James McDivitt
Virgil Grissom   Gordon Cooper   Frank Borman
John Glenn, Jr.   John Young   James Lovell, Jr.
Scott Carpenter

1. _____

_____

2. _____

_____

3. _____

_____

4. _____

_____

5. _____

_____

6. _____

_____

7. _____

_____

8. _____

_____

9. _____

_____

10. _____

_____

TIME

 ## KNOWLEDGE

List as many things as you can think of that help us measure time.

 ## COMPREHENSION

In your own words, explain the meanings of the following time-related proverbs. Give personal examples to illustrate your explanations.

a. A stitch in time saves nine.
b. Time should work for you, but not you for time.
c. Time -- the most valuable thing a person can spend.

 ## APPLICATION

Discover how long it will take a pendulum with a 50 foot string to make one complete revolution. Use a chart like the one below to help you find the answer. (Hint: Start with a shorter string.)

Length of string	Time

 ## ANALYSIS

Point out instances when it is and when it is not important to measure time very accurately.

 ## SYNTHESIS

Invent a new and unusual timepiece for each of the following individuals:

    Princess Diana   Superman   E.T.

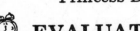 ## EVALUATION

Design a time capsule for people to open five hundred years from now. Your time capsule should include items that reflect this exact moment in time. Choose objects that would represent each category below. Then write why you think each object is a good choice.

your community   your environment
your country   yourself
your favorite recreation

TIME

NAME _____   DATE

A time line shows the sequence and relationship of events.
Draw a time line to illustrate the main events of your life.   _____

Think of something which. . .   _____

a. is timeless
b. loses value with time
c. time will change
d. time will not change

Determine the winners of the mind-stretching races below
without worrying about the clock.

A. WHICH IS FASTER AND WHY?   _____
   1. A jet plane or a bolt of lightning?
   2. A grasshopper or a jack rabbit?
   3. Swimming upstream or bicycling uphill?

B. WHICH IS SLOWER AND WHY?
   1. Riding a camel or paddling a canoe with only one
      oar?
   2. Toasting a marshmallow over a candle flame or
      slicing bread without a knife?
   3. A snail or melting butter?

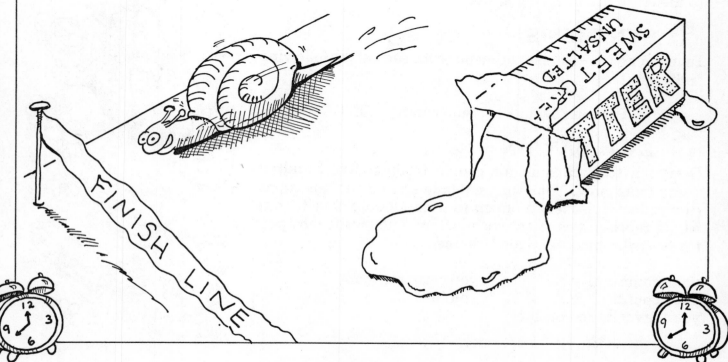

ON SCHEDULE

Write your daily schedule in the schedule box. After thinking carefully about the changes you would like to make, plan a new schedule. Draw hands on the clocks below to show the time for each major activity of the day and label the activities.

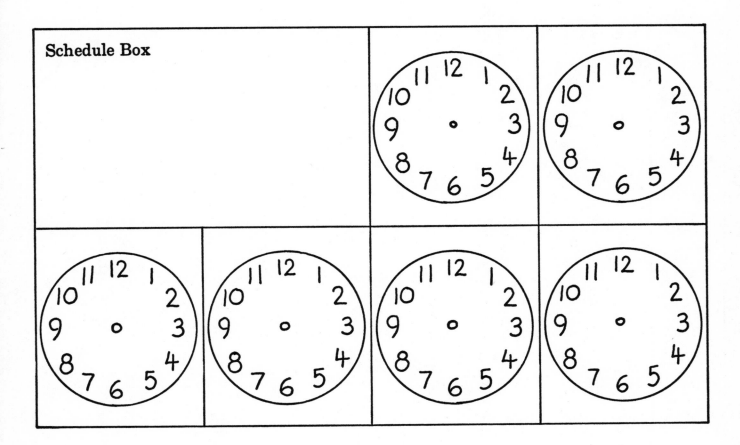

Make an X on the clock that shows the time of day that you enjoy most.

LIFE LINE

Make and illustrate a time line to show the events of your life from birth until the present. Use markers to write specific dates and to draw graphic details.

TORNADOES

KNOWLEDGE

Define the word tornado.

COMPREHENSION

Draw a picture to show the effects of a tornado.

APPLICATION

Outline a plan for protecting yourself from a tornado.

ANALYSIS

Compare the weather conditions that precede a tornado with the weather conditions that precede a snowstorm. How are the conditions alike and how are they different?

SYNTHESIS

Design a brochure to educate people about the dangers of a tornado.

EVALUATION

Which is more dangerous, a tornado or a hurricane? Write a paragraph to defend your position.

TORNADOES

NAME _____   DATE

Using the example below as a guide, what word clues
might you use to formulate the word tornado?   _____

   To rush   +   a stick used by old or   =   hurricane
  ("hurry")   crippled persons ("cane")

Every school has emergency plans for tornado warnings.
List the safety procedures for your school.   _____

Interview ten people, ranging in age from a twelve year old
to a senior citizen, to determine how many of them have
actually experienced a tornado. Graph your results.   _____

Make a filmstrip or design a story board about the
formation and destruction of a tornado and the safety
procedures to follow during a tornado.   _____

TORNADO ALERT

Unscramble the weather-related words and terms below.

1. aodornt _____

2. garniwn _____

3. tiwsret _____

4. dniw cteloviy _____

5. lunenf paedhs _____

6. oetnaeremm _____

7. retreuampet _____

8. dolusc _____

9. lage _____

10. spotmhacier resrpeus _____

11. aormteerb _____

12. ceofrtsa _____

13. tiasdsre _____

14. terpiptoicani _____

15. leroemtygoo _____

Write a paragraph describing the causes and effects of a tornado. Use at least ten of the unscrambled words in your paragraph.

_____

_____

_____

_____

_____

_____

_____

_____

_____

_____

_____

_____

Answer key on pages 126 and 127.

RECORD A TORNADO

Use reference materials to research the development, appearance, and effects of a tornado. Use the information to make a pictoral record of a tornado and its consequences.

1.	2.
3.	4.

TREES

 KNOWLEDGE

Complete this statement with as many reasons as you can think of.

"Trees are important to us because . . ."

 COMPREHENSION

Explain the role that trees play in the oxygen cycle.

 APPLICATION

Examine a tree in detail. Record your observations as to its size, color, bark, leaf design, branch arrangement, environment, distinguishing characteristics, and living inhabitants.

 ANALYSIS

Select a tree and one of its probable locations -- a palm tree in Florida, an evergreen in Maine, or a redwood in California. Make inferences about the events the tree might witness in its lifetime such as historical happenings, national catastrophes, ecological events, human progress, and everyday occurrences.

 SYNTHESIS

Suppose someone gave you one square mile of land and you were told that you could plant any kind of forest you wanted. What physical characteristics, climate, vegetation, animal life, and human values would your forest reflect?

 EVALUATION

What is the most important tree to mankind? Support your choice with facts.

TREES

NAME _____ DATE

List as many enemies of trees as you can think of. Group the list in several different ways.

_____

Read several poems about trees. Analyze these poems to discover what poets find so appealing about trees. Describe your findings.

_____

Pretend you are a tree. Write how you would feel in a forest fire, a hurricane, a lumber camp, a schoolyard, a national park, and a cemetery.

_____

Make a list of as many products as you can think of that are made from trees. Decide which of these products are necessities and which are luxuries.

_____

UNSCRAMBLE THE TREES

The names of 15 well-known trees are scrambled below. Unscramble the letters and write the names. Then write one distinguishing feature of each tree.

1. ppeal _ _ _ _ _ _____

2. totcnodwoo _ _ _ _ _ _ _ _ _ _____

_____

3. inpe _ _ _ _ _____

4. pamel _ _ _ _ _ _____

5. liwowl _ _ _ _ _ _ _____

6. amlp _ _ _ _ _____

7. raecd _ _ _ _ _ _____

8. oknggi _ _ _ _ _ _ _____

9. lme _ _ _ _____

10. ricbh _ _ _ _ _ _____

11. dleer _ _ _ _ _ _____

12. caymsroe _ _ _ _ _ _ _ _ _____

_____

13. dewodro _ _ _ _ _ _ _ _____

_____

14. senpa _ _ _ _ _ _____

15. tawlnu _ _ _ _ _ _ _____

_____

Answer key on pages 126 and 127.

WITHOUT TREES . . .

There would be . . .
no coffee, no cocoa, no tea,
no maple syrup or lemonade,
no cinnamon toast, nutmeg, or cloves,
no pineapple slices or pecan pie.
There wouldn't even be applesauce,
*   bananas, or orange juice.*

Without trees, kitchens would be dreary and dinners would be dull. Not just in the kitchen, but wherever people live and work, products from trees are important.

List three things that come from trees that can be found in the following places:

The classroom
1. _____
2. _____
3. _____

The lunchroom
1. _____
2. _____
3. _____

The bathroom
1. _____
2. _____
3. _____

ARE YOU ABLE TO LABEL THE PARTS OF A TREE?

Use the words in the word box to label the parts of the tree below. Then use a reference book to find the purpose of each of the parts.

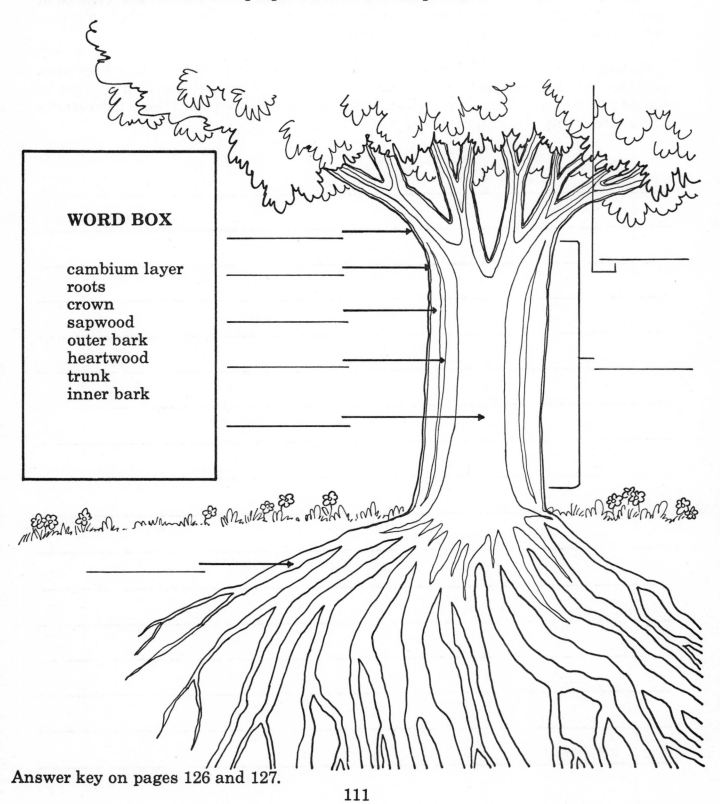

WORD BOX

cambium layer
roots
crown
sapwood
outer bark
heartwood
trunk
inner bark

Answer key on pages 126 and 127.

DANGER! TREES ARE AT STAKE

Trees around the world are constantly endangered by insects, diseases, and weather conditions. Human beings continue to be one of the chief enemies of trees. Millions of trees are cut down each year for wood and pulp. Likewise, many trees are destroyed by fires caused by human carelessness. In spite of the efforts of conservationists, forest rangers, and concerned citizens fighting for the protection of the world's endangered forests, the waste continues.

Collect information and develop an outline for a fifteen-minute radio or television program about forest safety for hikers, campers, or picnickers. Don't forget to include "attention getters", specific information, and examples of the consequences of not observing the program's advice.

_____

_____

_____

_____

_____

_____

_____

_____

_____

_____

_____

_____

_____

_____

TOPICAL OVERVIEW

EARTH SCIENCE

TOPIC	PROCESSES	GLOSSARY LISTINGS	
Ocean	generalizing problem solving recording information	brine coast continental slope currents marine ocean floor oceanographer oil spills	organism pesticides pollution salinity sewage tide toxic wastes wave
Rocks	comparing	minerals	
Time	experimenting graphing	pendulum revolution	
Tornadoes	comparing graphing outlining	hurricane tornado	

LIFE SCIENCE

Body systems	comparing	ailment body system cell corpuscle	disease muscle nerve ending
Environment	comparing outlining	cultural environment	environment- alist
Insects	classifying comparing graphing	bedbug dragonfly repellent	silverfish yellow jacket walking stick
Junk food	comparing drawing conclusions graphing	junk food	

TOPIC	PROCESSES	GLOSSARY LISTINGS	
Ocean	generalizing problem solving recording information	brine coast continental slope currents marine ocean floor oceanographer oil spills	organism pesticides pollution salinity sewage tide toxic wastes wave
Organ transplants	comparing experimenting	cornea donor liver	organ transplant
Plants	comparing drawing conclusions	scientific form	
Predators and prey	drawing conclusions	adaptations camouflage food chain	predator prey
Prehistoric life	classifying comparing predicting	adaptation carnivorous fossil fossil fuel	herbivorous paleontolo- gist prehistoric
Robots	comparing drawing conclusions	automation robot	
Senses	classifying comparing graphing	arch print Braille loop manual	Morse code optical illusion senses whorl
Trees	classifying making inferences observing	vegetation pulp conservationist	

PHYSICAL SCIENCE

TOPIC	PROCESSES	GLOSSARY LISTINGS	
Aviation	comparing constructing predicting rank-ordering	ailerons aviation cockpit dirigible drag elevators flaps fuselage gravity hang glider	helicopter hot air balloon landing gear lift parachute propeller rudder stabilizers thrust wings
Bicycle mechanics	inferring outlining	acceleration force friction gear	motion tandem velocipede velocity
Color	comparing experimenting graphing inferring	hue	
Endangered species	classifying outlining	endangered extinct	organism species
Space	comparing generalizing	astronaut constellations interplanetary mythology NASA	planets space star zodiac

ALL SCIENCES

TOPIC	PROCESSES	GLOSSARY LISTINGS	
Metric measure	measuring	centimeter decimeter	millimeter
Microscopes	experimenting	periscope spectroscope telescope	

DO-IT-YOURSELF OUTLINE FOR DEVELOPING A UNIT ON ANY SCIENCE TOPIC

Developing a science unit on a topic of your choice is easier than you think. Just choose your topic and then select one or more tasks from each level of Bloom's taxonomy (below) to create a teaching and learning unit.

TOPIC _____

KNOWLEDGE
1. List five to ten questions that you would like to answer about the topic.
2. Identify five to ten key words or terms related to the topic and write their definitions.
3. Name three to five specific sources for information about the topic.

COMPREHENSION
1. Outline a plan for finding out all you can about the topic.
2. Summarize what you would like to know most about the topic.
3. Describe five to ten ways that you might share acquired information.

APPLICATION
1. Interview someone with knowledge of the topic.
2. Make a model to show something important about the topic.
3. Conduct an experiment to demonstrate a key idea related to the topic.

ANALYSIS
1. Compare and contrast some aspect of your topic with that of another topic.
2. Divide your topic into several sub-topics.
3. Conduct a survey to show how others feel about the topic.

SYNTHESIS
1. Create a list of predictions related to the topic.
2. Compose a poem or story about the topic.
3. Design a series of drawings or diagrams to show facts about the topic.

EVALUATION
1. Determine the five most important facts you have learned about the topic. Rank order them from most important to least important, giving reasons for your first choice.
2. Criticize a resource you used to find out more information about the topic and give at least three recommendations for improving it.

REFERENCE GUIDE FOR DEVELOPING UNITS AND ACTIVITIES

STAGES

TRIGGER VERBS

KNOWLEDGE
recalling, restating, and
remembering learned
information

choose	label	read	what
find	list	recall	when
group	match	recite	where
identify	memorize	record	who
know	outline	select	write

COMPREHENSION
grasping meaning of
information by
interpreting and
translating learnings

associate	draw	group	show
change	estimate	outline	simplify
contrast	expand	reorganize	summarize
define	explain	retell	transform

APPLICATION
making use of
information in a context
different from the one in
which it was learned

apply	experiment	produce
choose	interview	prove
classify	model	record
construct	modify	select
employ	predict	utilize

ANALYSIS
breaking learned
information into its
component parts

analyze	discover	simplify
break down	divide	sort
classify	examine	survey
compare	infer	take apart
contrast	inspect	transform

SYNTHESIS
creating new
information and ideas
using previous learnings

blend	design	make up
build	devise	originate
combine	develop	predict
compose	form	produce
construct	imagine	rearrange
create	invent	suppose

EVALUATE
making judgments
about learned
information on basis of
established criteria

assess	determine	rank
award	evaluate	rate
conclude	grade	recommend
criticize	judge	select
decide	justify	support
defend	measure	test

117

EXPERIMENT FORM FOR USE WITH ANY SCIENCE TOPIC

KNOWLEDGE

List the materials used in this experiment.

Materials:

_____

_____

_____

_____

COMPREHENSION

Outline the procedure for conducting this experiment.

Procedure:

1. _____ 4. _____

2. _____ 5. _____

3. _____ 6. _____

APPLICATION

Record data observed and collected during your experiment in chart or graph form.

Data:

What I Did	What I Observed

ANALYSIS

Examine your data and draw conclusions.

Conclusions:

1. _____

_____

2. _____

_____

3. _____

_____

SYNTHESIS

Create a series of "what if" statements about your data to show things that might be different should variables be changed.

What if ... _____

_____

What if... _____

_____

What if... _____

_____

EVALUATION

Describe how you would rate the success of your experiment. Establish a set of criteria for measuring the results.

Findings	Measure of Success

BOOK REPORT OUTLINE FOR USE WITH ANY SCIENCE TOPIC

DIRECTIONS: Select a non-fiction book on the science topic of your choice and use it to complete the activities below.

KNOWLEDGE
1. Record the answers to each of these questions:
   What is the title of the book?
   Who wrote the book?
   When was the book published?
   Where did you locate the book?

COMPREHENSION
2. Summarize the main ideas or facts found in the book.

APPLICATION
3. Select several key words or terms from the book and classify them in some way.

ANALYSIS
4. Compare your book with another book on the same topic. How are the books alike and how are they different?

SYNTHESIS
5. Suppose that you were to write a new book on this topic. Create an original book jacket for your masterpiece.

EVALUATION
6. Would you recommend the book to anyone else? Give three to five reasons for your choice.

STUDENT PROFILE

Student	Activity	Date Started	Date Completed	Rating

Rating code: (1) non-satisfactory, (2) satisfactory, (3) good, (4) very good, (5) superior

GLOSSARY

acceleration - rate of change in speed of a moving object

adaptation - a change, feature, or characteristic that increases an organism's chances of survival

airplane parts -

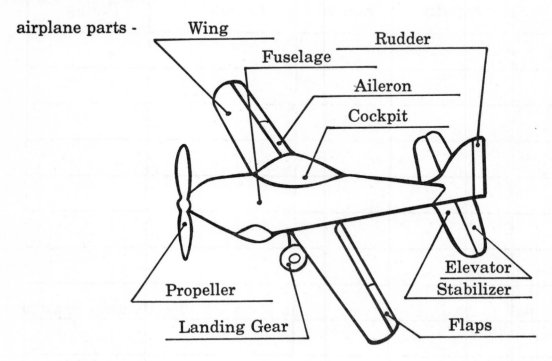

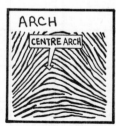

arch print - a fingerprint which has an arch pattern in the middle surrounded by arch-shaped ridges

attract - magnets are said to attract each other when two unlike magnetic poles are placed end to end causing the magnets to stick together

automation - a system by which equipment is used to make something act or operate without external or conscious control

brine - water containing large amounts of salt such as the water of the sea or ocean

camouflage - the method of hiding from an enemy by blending in with one's natural surroundings

carnivorous - a meat-eating organism

cell - a microscopic part of an animal

centimeter - 1/100 of a meter

coast - the land next to the sea; the seashore

compass - a tool for finding direction which consists of a magnetic needle that is free to move about until it is lined up with the magnetic field of the earth

constellation - a group of stars that form a pattern in the sky

cornea - the clear covering at the front of the eye

corpuscle - a free-moving blood cell

currents - streams of moving water below the ocean's surface

decimeter - 1/10 of a meter

drag - backward force which slows down an airplane while in flight; drag may be reduced by making air pass more smoothly across the airplane's surfaces

extinct - no longer in existence

food chain - a series of organisms in which each organism feeds on the organism below it

force - push or pull exerted on an object which gives the object energy to start moving, stop moving, or change its movement

fossil - any hardened remains or traces of plant or animal life found in rocks

friction - force that opposes the motion of an object

gear - the toothed wheel on an airplane

gravity - the pull of the earth

herbivorous - a plant-eating organism

hue - a shade or tint of a particular color

lift - the upward force of air on a moving object

loop - a fingerprint which has a center line shaped like a hairpin surrounded by ridges that repeat until they reach another shape called the delta

magnetic field - the pattern of magnetism around a magnet

millimeter - 1/1000 of a meter

motion - change in position

magnetic poles - the ends of a magnet

marine - related to the sea or ocean

ocean floor - the bottom of the ocean

oceanography - the exploration and scientific study of the ocean

oil spills - the accidental dumping of petroleum into the ocean

optical illusion - a visual image that is misleading

organism - any individual animal or plant that carries out all of the basic life functions

paleontologist - an individual who studies fossils

pendulum - an object suspended from a fixed support so as to swing freely back and forth under the influences of gravity

periscope - a tubular instrument containing a mirror or prism to permit observation from a spot or position out of the direct line of sight

pesticides - chemicals used to kill pests such as insects and rodents

pollution - unclean air or water

planet - a large body that revolves around the sun

predator - an organism that eats other organisms

prey - an organism that is hunted and eaten by another organism

pulp - a mixture of fine, moist cellulose material from which paper is made

repel - magnets are said to repel each other when two like magnetic poles are placed end to end causing the magnets to resist attraction

salinity - related to the salt content of a solution

seaweed - any sea plant or plants

sewage - liquid and solid waste matter carried off the ground water in sewers or drains

species - a group of organisms that are closely related to one another and, upon mating, can produce new organisms

spectroscope - an instrument that breaks light into its particular colors star - a heavenly body of gases seen as a fixed point of light in the night sky

telescope - an instrument which makes distant objects appear to be nearer and larger

tides - the daily rise and fall of the surface of the oceans and seas, and the bodies of water connected to them, caused by the attraction of the moon and sun

thrust - the forward force exerted by an airplane moving through the air

vegetation - any type of plant life

velocity - the speed and direction of motion

waves - pulses of energy that move through the water

whorl - a fingerprint which has a coiled line in the middle, either circular or oval, and a delta on each side

zodiac - twelve constellations which form a background of stars that the sun, moon, and planets pass through every year

Page 21

1. wheel
   crank hangcr
2. tire valve
   handle grips
3. warning device
   pedals
4. crank hanger
   chain
5. saddle
   light
6. handlebars
   fork

PUZZLING INSECTS

Find and circle the names of 30 insects in the word find puzzle below. The words may be spelled vertically or horizontally, but not diagonally or backward. Write every leftover letter, except the letters a, b, c, and d in the space below the puzzle. Unscramble the letters to spell the name of a professionally trained person who studies insects.

totsimeognlo
entomologist
44

Page 22

1. inspection
2. signal
3. pedestrian
4. intersection
5. bicycle
6. spokes
7. chain
8. brakes
9. grips
10. handlebars
11. pedals
12. reflector
13. bike route
14. crosswalk
15. warning signs

Page 53

centiliter	: cl
centimeter	: cm
decaliter	: dl
deciliter	: dl
gram	: g
hectogram	: hg
kilogram	: kg
liter	: l
meter	: m
milligram	: mg
millimeter	: mm
myriameter	: mym

Page 61

1. G
2. H
3. K
4. J
5. L
6. A
7. I
8. E
9. D
10. B
11. C
12. F

Page 71

1. D
2. F
3. G
4. I
5. H
6. A
7. J
8. C
9. E
10. B

UNDERCOVER INSECTS

Find and color nine insects hiding in the picture below. Can you name at least five insects that use camouflage as part of their protection?

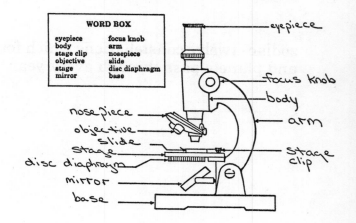

walking stick   treehopper
grasshopper   katydid   lantern fly   praying mantis
43

PAGE 57

MICRO MANIA

Use the words in the word box to label the parts of the microscope below.

WORD BOX

eyepiece	focus knob
body	arm
stage clip	nosepiece
objective	slide
stage	disc diaphragm
mirror	base

eyepiece
focus knob
body
arm
nosepiece
objective
slide
stage clip
disc diaphragm
mirror
base

HIDDEN PREY

Find and color the following animals hiding in the picture below.

mouse   frog   rooster   worm   rabbit   deer   chipmunk   fly

Then draw a line from each prey to a predator from which it could be hiding. Some animals may be hiding from more than one predator, so select the predator that you think would be most likely seeking each prey.

Draw pictures to add one more predator and its prey to the picture.
78

DINOSAURS IN HIDING

Five dinosaurs are hiding in the picture below. Find and color the dinosaurs and write each dinosaur's name underneath the picture.

Select the dinosaur that interests you most and write a report about it. Write the report so that it could be used as an article for a natural history magazine. Be sure to include complete bibliographical information for all reference materials used.

Pteranodon   Tyrannosaurus
Stegosaurus   Diplodocus   Polacanthus
79

True: 1, 2, 4, 5, 8
False: 3, 6, 7, 9

80

PAGE 93

THE EYES HAVE IT

Use the words in the word box to label the parts of the eye.

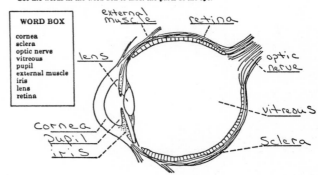

WORD BOX

cornea
sclera
optic nerve
vitreous
pupil
external muscle
iris
lens
retina

PAGE 89

ROCK-A-ROUND

Complete the crossword puzzle.

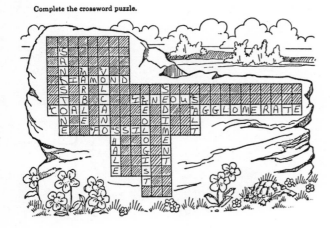

ARE YOU ABLE TO LABEL THE PARTS OF A TREE?

Use the words in the word box to label the parts of the tree below. Then use a reference book to find the purpose of each of the parts.

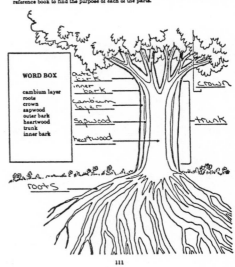

WORD BOX

cambium layer
roots
crown
sapwood
outer bark
heartwood
trunk
inner bark

111

Page 105	Page 109
1. tornado	1. apple
2. warning	2. cottonwood
3. twister	3. pine
4. wind velocity	4. maple
5. funnel shaped	5. willow
6. anemometer	6. palm
7. temperature	7. cedar
8. clouds	8. ginkgo
9. gale	9. elm
10. atmospheric pressure	10. birch
11. barometer	11. elder
12. forecast	12. sycamore
13. disaster	13. redwood
14. precipitation	14. aspen
15. meteorology	15. walnut